MASTERS OF WORLD PAINTING

Henri Matisse

HARRY N. ABRAMS, INC., PUBLISHERS, NEW YORK
AURORA ART PUBLISHERS, LENINGRAD

COMPILED AND INTRODUCED BY ALBERT KOSTENEVICH

TRANSLATED FROM THE RUSSIAN BY MONICA WILKINSON
AND PETER WALDRON

DESIGNED BY VIACHESLAV BAKHTIN

Library of Congress Catalog Card Number: 80-67463
International Standard Book Number: 0-8109-2240-1

Created by Aurora Art Publishers, Leningrad,
for joint publication of Aurora and Harry N. Abrams, Inc., New York

PRINTED AND BOUND IN THE USSR

In 1896, at the age of twenty-six, Matisse made his artistic debut in the Salon de la Société Nationale des Beaux-Arts. At that time the artist was painting mainly still lifes, but also some landscapes and interior scenes with figures; he was still attending Gustave Moreau's classes in the Ecole des Beaux-Arts and painstakingly copying the masterpieces in The Louvre, though he had already begun to feel that he was more than a mere pupil.

When we look at *The Bottle of Schiedam* (1896, The Pushkin Museum of Fine Arts, Moscow), the earliest of Matisse's works in Soviet museums, we are forcibly reminded of how long he spent in The Louvre, both by himself and under the tutelage of Moreau. This work was undoubtedly painted under the spell of Chardin's still lifes, for not only is each object delicately fashioned in the Chardin style, but his influence is felt in the very choice and positioning of the objects. Here Matisse was conforming to classical standards, as was expected of a student of the Ecole des Beaux-Arts. Nothing in the strict pyramidal composition of the painting, its restrained color range, or the careful attention paid to half-tones, reflections, and shadows heralds the rebellion that was soon to be a talking point among artists and connoisseurs all over Europe. But even when Matisse subsequently rejected the use of half-tones and shadows, in order to attain a perfect beauty and intensity of color, he never infringed upon the foundations of art: whatever artistic language Matisse used in his works, he constantly searched for harmony, lively rhythm, and lucid form. Matisse's "identity" is already evident in *The Bottle of Schiedam*, which scrupulously follows the manner of the traditional still life — although it is not yet clear what direction the artist's search will take.

Each of the objects in the picture is recognizable at first glance, and the viewer's eye moves easily between the different planes of the still life. The tablecloth falling in folds from the table appears to coincide with the plane of the picture and becomes the starting point for the three-dimensional construction of space. In order to create an illusion of depth the other items are designed to transcend this plane. The knife handle protruding slightly from the edge of the table seems to penetrate into the space beyond the canvas and looks almost as if we could pick it up. At the same time the blade draws our attention to the central plane of the composition, where the bottle of Schiedam, almost merging into the background, reigns alone. The idea implicit in this still life is that, for all its enigmas, the world is orderly and rational.

The objects that the young Matisse depicted are not extravagant, but neither are they banal; just such things would always attract the artist and reappear in picture after picture. The black bottle of Dutch vodka, an object of casual but noble beauty, figures in two other still lifes done by Matisse before the Moscow painting. Nevertheless, we shall not dwell here on the external aspect of familiar objects, but instead concentrate on the essential, innermost elements of Matisse's art.

The starting point of Matisse's work is obviously the art of the Old Masters. But the artist could not maintain this attitude for long. The visible world, it seemed to him, had been studied sufficiently, and neither perspective nor chiaroscuro — both tested methods of artistic penetration into the secrets of the visible world — promised new discoveries. Moreover, the fact that the objective characteristics of the external world could be studied more effectively by photography was bound to make the artist concentrate on qualities and approaches not dependent on mechanical perception, the most important of which was his personal attitude to the world around him. Many years later, when Matisse was asked why he was an artist, he replied: "To translate my emotions, my feelings and the reactions of my sensibility into color and design, something that neither the most perfect camera, even in colors, nor the cinema can do. . . . We need only those painters who have the gift to translate their intimate feelings into color and design" (Alfred H. Barr, Jr., *Matisse: His Art and His Public*, New York: Museum of Modern Art, 1951, p. 562).

Matisse worked out this attitude in the last years of the nineteenth century. Soon after painting a number of pictures similar to *The Bottle of Schiedam* he discovered for himself the art of the Impressionists, under whose influence he began to purify his palette. However, the Impressionists' gravitation toward an objective visual perception of the world was alien to him. The series of still lifes in The Hermitage in Leningrad, dating from 1897 to 1900, clearly shows how Matisse's search for a style, one that would enable him to express deeply personal feelings in the most energetic manner, rapidly drew the artist away from the Impressionists toward Van Gogh and Gauguin. The objects in his pictures, so quiet and unpretentious only a short time before, began to sparkle defiantly with broad strokes of pure color, expressing tension and aroused emotions.

Matisse understood very soon, however, that the stronger the emotion the greater was the necessity of using reason to dam its flow, and became convinced that the only intermediary capable of conveying the artist's emotions to others was the world around him, and them — from insignificant everyday items to trees and hills, from the bodies of his models to the faces of his friends and relatives. Since, in his opinion, the artist's emotions could best be revealed to the viewer through these most ordinary things, such things should always be easily recognizable.

The trees in *The Luxembourg Gardens* of 1901 (The Hermitage, Leningrad) are no more than simplified patches of dense color which, though much more intense than anything seen in nature, does in fact stem from nature. The trees are therefore not only easily recognizable, but evoke the atmosphere of early autumn with its particularly chilly shade and the unexpected juxtaposition of the as yet lush, thick greenery and the yellow glades and bright red leaves.

Matisse was a son of the nineteenth century in that he retained an unshakable attachment to nature throughout his life. But the transformations of nature he achieved by his use of color and line recall not so much the work of nineteenth-century artists, or even those of the sixteenth to eighteenth centuries, but rather the creations of medieval and oriental masters. Only beyond the historical (and geographical) bounds of modern Europe could Matisse find color of a quality similar to that he was striving for: pure, powerful, and open, without a trace of chiaroscuro. Color began to exert such a magical sway over him that he would not sacrifice it even for all the achievements of the Renaissance. But in returning to the long-neglected pre-Renaissance coloristic tradition Matisse was of course not thinking of a return to medieval artistic subjects. His was an earthly art, deeply permeated with real impressions and full of contemporary passions. The sunny, temperamental canvases of 1905—1907, which gave both sense and stimulus to the Fauvist movement, embody the jubilant and rebellious energy of the new century, its hopes and its uncompromising nature.

What the visitors to the Salon d'Automne of 1905 and to other Fauvist exhibitions saw only as a challenge and a desire to shock turned out to be an authentically sincere, perhaps rather naive, but pure expression of a turbulent young thirst for life the likes of which had not been seen before.

One of the most radiant works of Fauvist art is *View of Collioure* (1906, The Hermitage), a joyful paean to Mediterranean sunshine. Although almost childishly simple, this landscape required considerable knowledge of the principles laid down by Cézanne, Van Gogh, and Gauguin, that great trio of Post-Impressionists. The least obvious link is perhaps that with Cézanne, the artist Matisse respected above all others. The blazing colors of the Collioure landscape make us forget that the picture is based on a drawing reflecting his perception of Cézanne. However, the impression that it was done spontaneously, without any preliminary work, is deceptive. The paints are applied to the canvas quickly and impetuously, but this was undoubtedly preceded by an interval in which the artist, deep in thought, with pencil in hand, set out the position of each object in fine lines — which later almost vanished under the avalanche of color — a method used by Matisse in his later works.

Like Van Gogh and Gauguin, Matisse strove for maximum dynamism of color, and to this end used the device of juxtaposing contrasting tones. By giving color autonomy Matisse of course went further along this path than his predecessors, but what is less obvious is that Matisse's boldest experiments with color arose from his penetration into the essence of nature. Beyond a doubt, Matisse depended on nature more than Gauguin, Van Gogh, or the Neo-Impressionists. It is sufficient to examine the role of brushstrokes in a picture like *View of Collioure.* In his synthetism, Gauguin was tempted to sacrifice the effect of brushstrokes in order to create wide, quiet areas of color; Van Gogh's impetuous, curving strokes, on the other hand, were forced insofar as they expressed, first and foremost, emotional impulses. During his work in Collioure in the summers of 1905 and 1906, Matisse, it seems, still did not wish to forget the lessons of the Neo-Impressionists and thus always used separate brushstrokes. The way in which he applied the brush, however, was completely different from the technique of, say, Paul Signac, whose mosaic method involved totally level brushstrokes and whose monotonous "brushstroke-bricks" were necessary only as far as they enabled him to create a play of color. Matisse's brushstrokes are more varied than Signac's or Van Gogh's, and while it is impossible to deny their emotional quality, they are also used to achieve concrete pictorial effects. Thus, the alternations of brushstrokes and unpainted priming are designed to conjure up the sparkling of the tiled roofs and ripples of the sea under the midday sun. Consequently, these alternations are functional and the painting cannot be considered "unfinished."

In *View of Collioure* the colors are as condensed and purified as the artist's feelings are concentrated. The actual colors of a noonday in the Mediterranean are different, for under the scorching sun they lose their strength and become whitish. Matisse, the color-worshipper, could not allow this, and would not even dream of creating an illusion of authentic lighting, for then color would play a secondary role. He believed that color by itself could express everything he needed, and his colors indeed convey magnificently the burning southern heat — not the kind of heat that saps one's strength (there would be no poetry in that!) but a luxurious sultriness.

The years 1906 and 1907, when *Bouquet, Lady on the Terrace* (both in The Hermitage), and other pictures were painted, were the golden years of Fauvism, when Matisse, intoxicated with color, was often inclined to throw caution to the winds. However, he quickly realized that wealth and power of color *could* be created not by piling on dense, supercharged paints but, on the contrary, by using them sparingly. In *Nude. Black and Gold* or *Nymph and Satyr* (1908 and 1909, both in The Hermitage) — pictures startling in their coloristic simplicity — the artist merely juxtaposes two dominant colors, which are only slightly modulated and supported by one or two secondary muted shades.

Matisse was not the first to compare the bare skin of a nude with gold. Gauguin had made a similar analogy in the work *And the Gold of Their Bodies* (1901, The Louvre, Paris). Both Matisse and Gauguin had an exalted poetic approach to this theme, and used color as the main means of attaining their goal. The difference between the two is that Matisse, in resorting to exaggeration, did not feel a need to justify himself by using exotic motifs when he gave his pictures terser and bolder color. Surely a human body can be depicted simply in ocher and black? With Matisse plain ocher becomes a jewel, for in close proximity with black it is shot with gold. It is difficult to name another artist who made this color so expressive and bold.

Nude. Black and Gold is extremely simple. It is not a programmatic work based on some specific subject or preconceived idea, but merely a study of the artist's model standing in an ordinary relaxed pose. However, it was obviously not by chance that Matisse selected this canvas as one of the four illustrations in his *Notes of a Painter*, the manifesto of the new French painting and one of the most amazing treatises that ever came from an artist's pen. *Nude. Black and Gold* is marked by powerful architectonic drawing and a frugal but expressive color scale. It is one of a number of studies featuring the same model and dating from 1908. She is portrayed in the same pose in a canvas called *Nude* (The Hermitage), which Matisse gave to the artist Ilya Ostroukhov, who accompanied him on his walks around Moscow. A comparison of the two pictures shows how much long, painstaking effort the artist must have put into this modest motif, so that eventually his depiction of the professional model lost its commonplace aspect and she became an object of worship for some unknown, awe-inspiring, albeit very earthly cult.

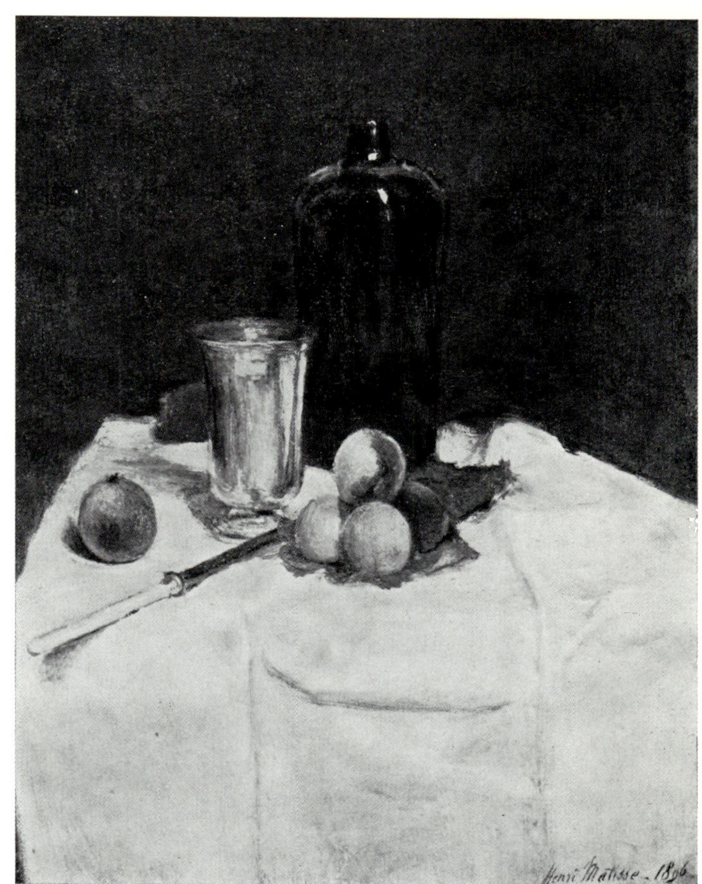

The Bottle of Schiedam. 1896
Oil on canvas. $28^3/_4 \times 23^5/_8$″ (73 × 60 cm)
The Pushkin Museum of Fine Arts, Moscow

From then on Matisse, now a mature painter, felt an urge to undertake truly significant works; he realized that he was capable of painting large, monumental canvases. But representatives of official Salon art, who at the 1896 Salon had been ready to treat him quite favorably, did not now wish to hear a word about this dauber who flouted established artistic conventions. The artist who could have revived monumental painting — which had gone into a complete decline — was to remain an easel painter.

At the beginning of the twentieth century only a few people were interested in acquiring a Matisse, and many years were to pass before national museums started buying his pictures. Happily it was just at this time, perhaps the most crucial period in his creative life, that he gained the support of a keen, perceptive collector. This was the Moscow merchant Sergei Shchukin, who devoted his life to collecting

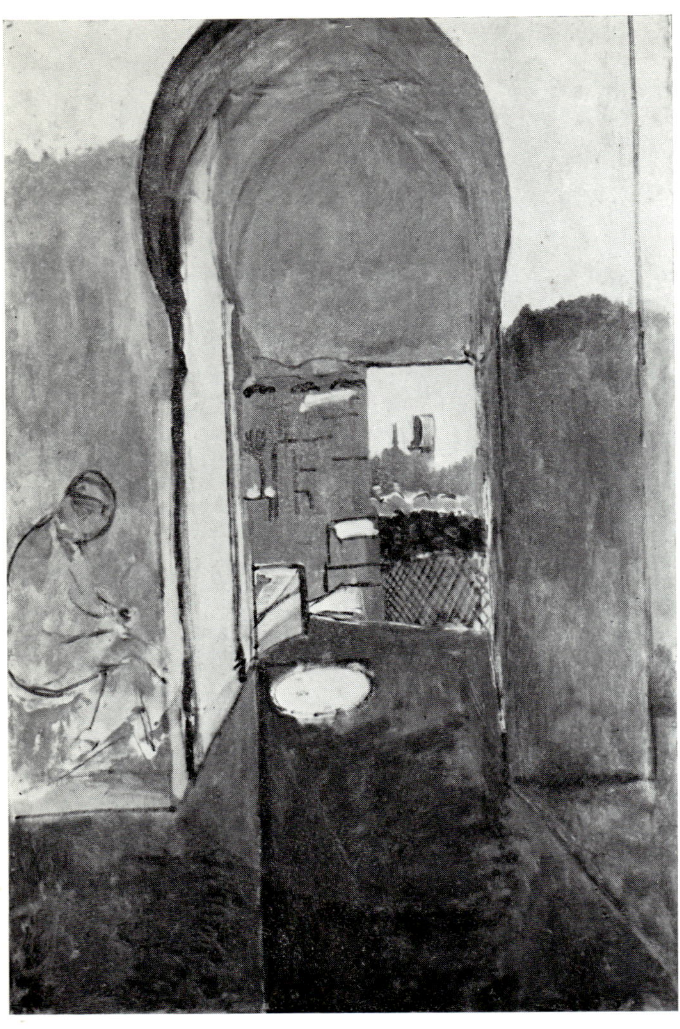

Entrance to the Casbah. 1912
Oil on canvas. $45^5/_8 \times 31^1/_2$″ (116 × 80 cm)
The Pushkin Museum of Fine Arts, Moscow

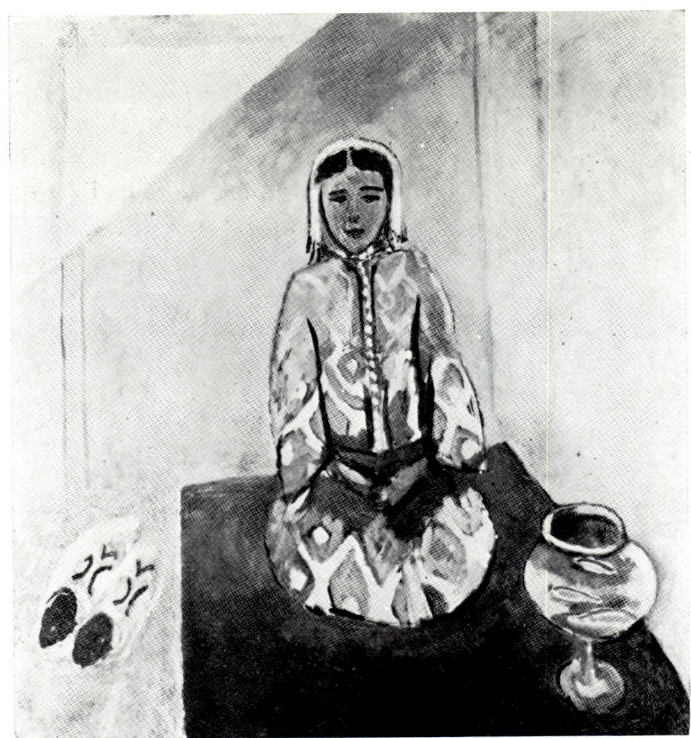

Zorah on the Terrace. 1912
Oil on canvas. $45^5/_8 \times 39^3/_8$″ (116 × 100 cm)
The Pushkin Museum of Fine Arts, Moscow

works by contemporary Western European artists, French in particular. It is thanks to him above all that the Soviet collection of Matisses in The Hermitage in Leningrad and The Pushkin Museum of Fine Arts in Moscow is justly considered one of the best in the world. *The Dance, Music,* and *The Red Room* were all painted for Shchukin, and also among the thirty-seven Matisses that he owned were such masterpieces as *Conversation, Spanish Woman with Tambourine, Satyr and Nymph, The Artist's Family, Goldfish, Arab Coffeehouse,* and *Portrait of the Artist's Wife.* Without these canvases any evaluation of Matisse's work would be unthinkable.

The harmonious and trusting relations which evolved between Matisse and Shchukin encouraged the artist to completely rework *Harmony in Blue. Decorative Panel for a Dining Room,* first exhibited at the Salon d'Automne of 1908. The focal point of the picture was the beautiful blue *toile de Jouy* often depicted in the artist's still lifes; for example, in *Blue Tablecloth* (1909, The Hermitage). In *Harmony in Blue,* Matisse was so captivated by this cloth that he covered the table and wall with it, and made every detail, from the figure of the woman laying the table to the trees in the garden, subordinate to the rhythms and lines dictated by its pattern (which, of course, is in reality less dynamic than it appears in Matisse's work). At the beginning of 1909, when the picture had already been bought by Shchukin but was still in Matisse's studio, he suddenly decided to repaint it as *Harmony in Red* or *The Red Room* or *La Desserte* (1908—1909, The Hermitage).

In what is seemingly a reference to this transformation in reverse, Matisse once said: "One can change a red, green, blue, and black surface into a different one in white, blue, red, and green; it remains the same picture with the same feeling to it, only presented in a different way, but the rhythms change. The difference between the two canvases is the same as the different position of chessmen at two different stages of a game" (*Matisse: Ecrits et propos sur l'art,* ed. Dominique Fourcade. Paris: Hermann, 1972, p. 132).

There were two reasons why this bold and drastic change of the entire color scheme was possible. First, since Matisse had been using pure colors for quite some time, he had acquired a deep understanding of their interaction. Second, in *Harmony in Blue* and, consequently, in *The Red Room* he was tackling a theme very familiar to him. In 1896 and 1897 Matisse had painted a room with a servant by a table in *Breton Maid* and *Dinner Table* (private collections). He was trying even then to follow two alternative

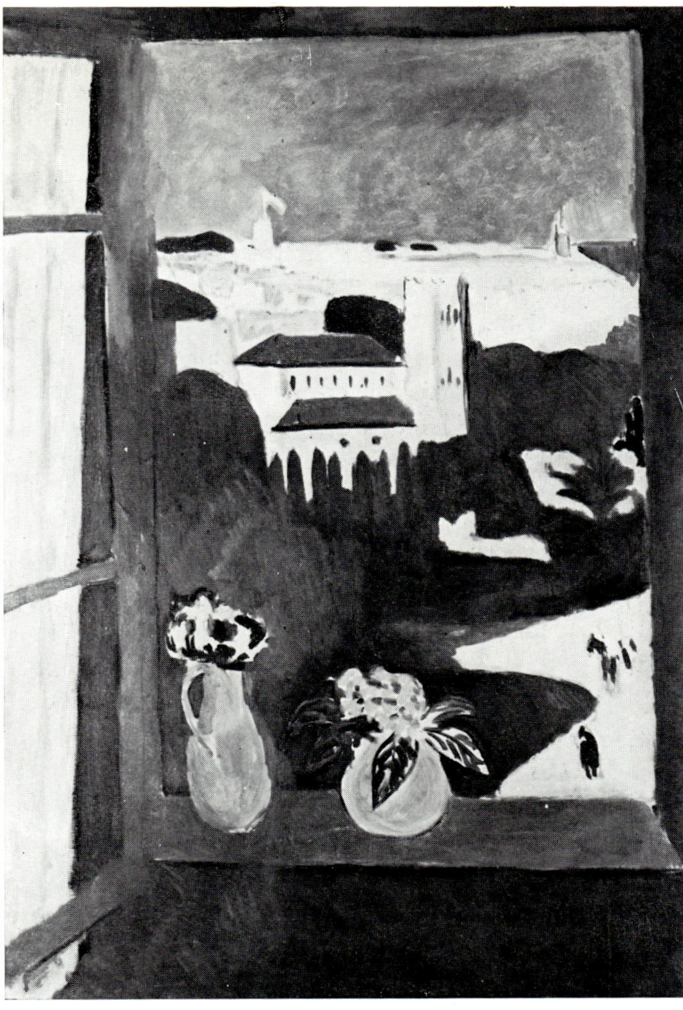

View from a Window. Tangier. 1912
Oil on canvas. $45^5/_8 \times 31^1/_2''$ (116×80 cm)
The Pushkin Museum of Fine Arts, Moscow

paths which had for two generations beckoned French artists: that of psychological realism on the one hand and that of picturesque impressionism on the other. Matisse realized that the time for quiet interior scenes had passed, and so he dispensed with them once and for all in *The Red Room.* The world was on the threshold of immense upheavals that nobody could foresee and that could be captured only by the artist's intuition. The "panel for a dining room" became a far from innocent decoration. The peaceful room — the woman moving unhurriedly around and the elegant still life — underwent a metamorphosis, condensing into a proud, challenging composition that stuns the viewer like the sounding of a great gong. *The Red Room* expressed the spirit of the coming era with unusual power and simplicity.

Apparently in the same year, 1909, Matisse began to work on *Conversation* (The Hermitage), another programmatic piece no less bold than *The Red Room.* Although these two canvases produce different impressions (the red and blue are perceived differently), they are related to one another. Of almost identical dimensions, they are invested with a poster-like vividness which is created by the resolute predominance of a single color. If Western European artists had never produced anything that incorporated so much red as *The Red Room,* then no picture before *Conversation* had contained such a concentration of blue. True, Picasso had already passed through his Blue Period a good five years before, but even his largest blue works are smaller than *Conversation* and, more important, they display a far more uniform application of and purpose for color; in Picasso's blue works the designation of color is frankly symbolic. To Picasso the deliberate charging of a picture with blue, where objects seem covered by a film of blue glass, signifies that life is full of grief and misery, and that the more miserable it is the more spiritual potential his personages have. Matisse's blue *Conversation* is much more coherent, not simply because the juxtaposition of various pure colors — green, black, and pink — lends it more life, but also because it has a dual nature, both real and ideal.

Indeed, the blue element enveloping the two figures is both a kind of "ideal" substance (which embodies the concentration of thought) and a more concrete indication of the shadowiness of the room, insofar as both figures are seen in half-shadow. The Impressionists were the first to discover how captivatingly blue shadows are. Without the Impressionists a picture like *Conversation* would have been impossible, although they themselves would probably have been deeply surprised to see the result of their discoveries. In his work Gauguin had already gone to extremes and imparted a timeless quality to the nuances that the Impressionists had used to fix transient conditions. Matisse was even more radical in this respect. That is why the blue shadow of his *Conversation* is not a shadow as such. It becomes a bridge linking two worlds: the physical, in which all illuminated objects cast shadows, and the spiritual, to which the artist's emotions belong.

In many of his paintings Matisse tries to show not so much objects themselves as the interrelationships between them. Therefore, his objects are not meant to cast actual shadows, for these are appropriate if it is necessary to create the illusion of "real" space on canvas. But Matisse worked on the premise that since canvas is a plane surface, this feeling of flatness should be preserved in the finished work. He considered that the viewer did not need simply a mirror image of reality, but that a work of art should have more exalted aims than the mere copying of objects from the external world. In *Conversation* even the window aperture opening onto the garden does not cut through the plane. In order to obtain such an effect Matisse depicts the lawn in a flat, simplified manner, breaking it up with patches of blue that reconcile the window aperture with the foreground (though, of course, to refer to foreground and background in this case is purely conventional).

A century earlier, the open window had been one of the favorite motifs of the Romantics. It allowed them to make a strong distinction between the humdrum daily round and the poetry of infinity, which opens up alluring vistas and rings with the promise of spiritual liberation. It is precisely in the open window motif that the contraposition of "here" and "there," fundamental to Romantic aesthetics, found its most articulate expression, and thus the theme was naturally not fated to survive Romanticism. The dream separated from the reality of "here" and transmitted to the illusory "there" could not hold its charm forever.

One condition necessary for the revival of this old motif was the removal of the Romantic antinomy. The artist in love with the world around him discovers the spiritual and infinite in the most ordinary things, or, to be more exact, endows these things with his own spirituality. Compared with the Romantics of the early nineteenth century there is no discord in his soul; in any case, there is no room for it in his work.

What could be more commonplace than the situation depicted in *Conversation*? It is morning, and a man who has just got up and is still in his pajamas is being asked a question by his wife. In Matisse's interpretation this scene acquires a truly monumental greatness and an exalted poetic sense. Once again the most concrete aspects of life (for this is a portrait of Matisse and his wife) are linked to the abstract and general, and the characters become actors in an almost mythological scene. *Conversation* is Matisse's only painting about the union of man and woman.

The centerpiece of the composition is a railing based on one seen by Matisse in Issy-les-Moulineaux, where the picture was painted. The image of the railing stresses the two artistic principles used in depicting the male and female figures. The man is formed of straight lines, down to the stripes on his pajamas, while the woman is delineated in rounded though still rather rigid lines. It is precisely these two principles that give life to the picture. The tree that stands between the two figures fuses the straight and rounded shapes. Painted after a tree in the garden at Issy, it symbolizes here the tree of life.

Matisse's large decorative canvases of 1908—10 reveal not merely his temperament and unshakable desire to finally liberate color, but also his attitude toward the work of his contemporaries. It was not, however, Salon, or academic, art that Matisse was confronting; that was already dead and not worth struggling with. Matisse rejected such painters as Maurice Denis, who was riding high on the crest of the Art Nouveau wave, and who had enjoyed great success with, for example, his series of panels *The Story of Psyche*, produced in 1908 for the Moscow collector Ivan Morozov.

Hidden rivalries came to the surface in the Salon d'Automne of 1910, where *The Dance* and *Music* (both in The Hermitage) by Matisse were shown along with *The Dances* and *Cantata* by Denis. The similarity of subjects, although scarcely coincidental, made it easier for the public and the critics to compare the two artists. The gentle color, elegant lines, and refined movements in Denis' works all conformed to the tastes of the majority of experts. Matisse's paintings, on the other hand, were received so coldly that even Shchukin almost changed his mind about acquiring them. It took time for people to realize that the decorative ensemble of *The Dance* and *Music* marked a turning point in modern European art.

In the spring of 1909, when the panels were commissioned by Shchukin, Matisse explained the idea behind the compositional arrangement of *The Dance* and *Music* in an interview: "I have the task of decorating an atelier with three floors. In my mind's eye I see a visitor entering it from the outside and seeing the ground floor. I must awaken in him a desire to exert himself, and to do so I must convey a sensation of lightness and ease. My first panel depicts a round dance on a hilltop. By the time the guest reaches the first-floor landing he is well inside the house, whose silent spirit is embodied in a circle of people, some making music and some listening attentively" (*Matisse: Ecrits et propos sur l'art*, p. 62). Matisse had already depicted a background ring of six dancing figures in *The Joy of Living* (1905—1906) and by the beginning of 1909 he was working on the first version of *The Dance*, now in The Museum of Modern Art in New York.

Although the second version retains the original composition, the already dynamic colors are greatly intensified: the light blue takes on a rich dark hue and the pink becomes almost red. Very likely the new, more dazzling color scheme was necessary to convey the tempestuous nature of the dance, but it also reflected a clearer concept of the work as a whole.

Both *The Dance* and *Music* were created in keeping with an established tradition. For Matisse's immediate predecessors, the Symbolists, the round dance had become a rather hackneyed motif. The dance theme had occurred in the classics of European art from Mantegna and Cranach to Goya; the motif of music-making in the open air also had frequently attracted artists, beginning with the Renaissance. But, whereas in the dancing and playing figures depicted by the Old Masters and the Salon painters of the turn of the century one can easily recognize the artists' contemporaries (usually idealized), Matisse's figures must have been seen as caricatures.

It is difficult to say either that the characters in *The Dance* and *Music* were in fact the artist's contemporaries or that he had used them to express his ideas about his contemporaries. They are stripped not only of their clothes, but also of any attributes of time, except for the flute and violin. They are not aware of their nakedness and act not as would people from some historical period but rather as mythical personages. When these two paintings appeared, some critics took the characters to be representations of primitive man. But that approach led nowhere, for Matisse's panels had nothing in common with the so-called historical pictures of the Paris Salons, which presented the life of prehistoric savages as an archaeological "costume ball." It would have been difficult for the audiences at the 1910 Salon to come to terms with *The Dance* and *Music* even if they had been told that Matisse's characters should be seen not as historical but rather as symbolic. The Symbolists had accustomed them to a very different type of imagery.

The Joy of Living, in the Barnes Foundation in Merion, Pennsylvania, a painting which marked the beginning of that trend in Matisse's work which includes *A Game of Bowls*, *Satyr and Nymph*, and particularly the panels in The Hermitage, depicts a dream about a primeval golden age, a dream that had excited the imagination of many generations. However, a major artist cannot dream for too long, for he reflects willy-nilly the passions of his time, and conveys its rhythm. The tense sternness of *The Dance* and *Music*, which appeared inexplicable and wild in 1910, was perceived very differently after the great upheavals that took place in the decade that followed.

The people in Matisse's panels create art — and not just because they dance, sing, and play. They abandon themselves to the dancing and music with the same passion as that with which an artist gives himself to his work. The underlying theme can be seen as the interaction of man and life through the medium of art. It is obvious that for Matisse such a theme had immense significance and that he did not intend to limit himself by purely decorative aims.

It is naive to explain *The Dance*, as some critics have done, as purely an impression of the farandole in the Moulin de la Galette or of the sardana in Collioure. The meaning of the picture is much deeper than it appears at first glance. By transferring the action to the distant mythical dawn of humanity, Matisse created a vivid image full of profound symbolism.

In prehistoric times, dances were an expression of magic, an ancient act of creation embodying the triumph of life over death. Matisse himself defined dance as "life and rhythm." Experts on symbolism in ancient cultures have noted that dances in which people link hands signify the union of earth and sky. In Matisse's work the earth and sky do not serve simply as a background, but are actually participants in the action; their symbolic meaning is stressed by their intensified, simplified colors. The identical color scheme of both panels is neither coincidental nor merely designed to enhance their decorative unity: it underlines the universal nature of earth and sky. In both works the action is taking place on a hill. Hills or mountains have traditionally symbolized the unity of earth and sky and were therefore associated with ascension into the spiritual world.

When music and dance were treated symbolically in painting, in particular during the Middle Ages, the themes often incorporated the concept of a universal harmony. Matisse, on the other hand, handled the motif of the unity of earth and sky by means of an earthly theme; it can hardly have been by chance that the artist reduced the number of dancing women to five (in *The Joy of Living* there were six), for this is a number to which man has always attached a special importance — five fingers, five bodily extremities, etc. The influence of Christianity can also be felt here. In his work *Music*, Matisse again used five characters, so that the total number of people in the panels would be ten, a number signifying completeness and perfection.

Taken separately, *The Dance* and *Music* do not fully reveal the artist's intentions, but together they form a dialectical unity of opposites. In conformity with certain turn-of-the-century philosophical ideas, woman appears here as the personification of unity, whereas man embodies individualism. The two sexes war with each other and seek union at one and the same time. *Music* is as static as *The Dance* is full of movement; all the figures are as totally separated in *Music* as they are united in *The Dance*. *Music* was a difficult piece of work for Matisse. When he was already well into painting it, he twice altered the position of the figures. The contours of various details, later painted over, show through if the picture is examined closely; thus, a dog which was lying by the feet of the violin player obviously harked back to the theme of Orpheus, whose music entranced animals. The overall reworking of the panel was intended not only to render it more laconic, but also to make it diametrically opposed to *The Dance*. The plump woman once in the top right-hand corner was replaced by a singing youth; this change gave *Music* a male orientation, whereas females dominate *The Dance*.

"What I dream about," wrote Matisse in *Notes of a Painter*, "is a well-balanced, pure, tranquil art free of excitement and stimulation, which for those who work with their minds, businessmen or men of letters, is a relaxation, a respite from cerebral activity, something akin to a comfortable armchair in which a man rests his tired body." Of course, not every Matisse canvas complies with this artistic credo,

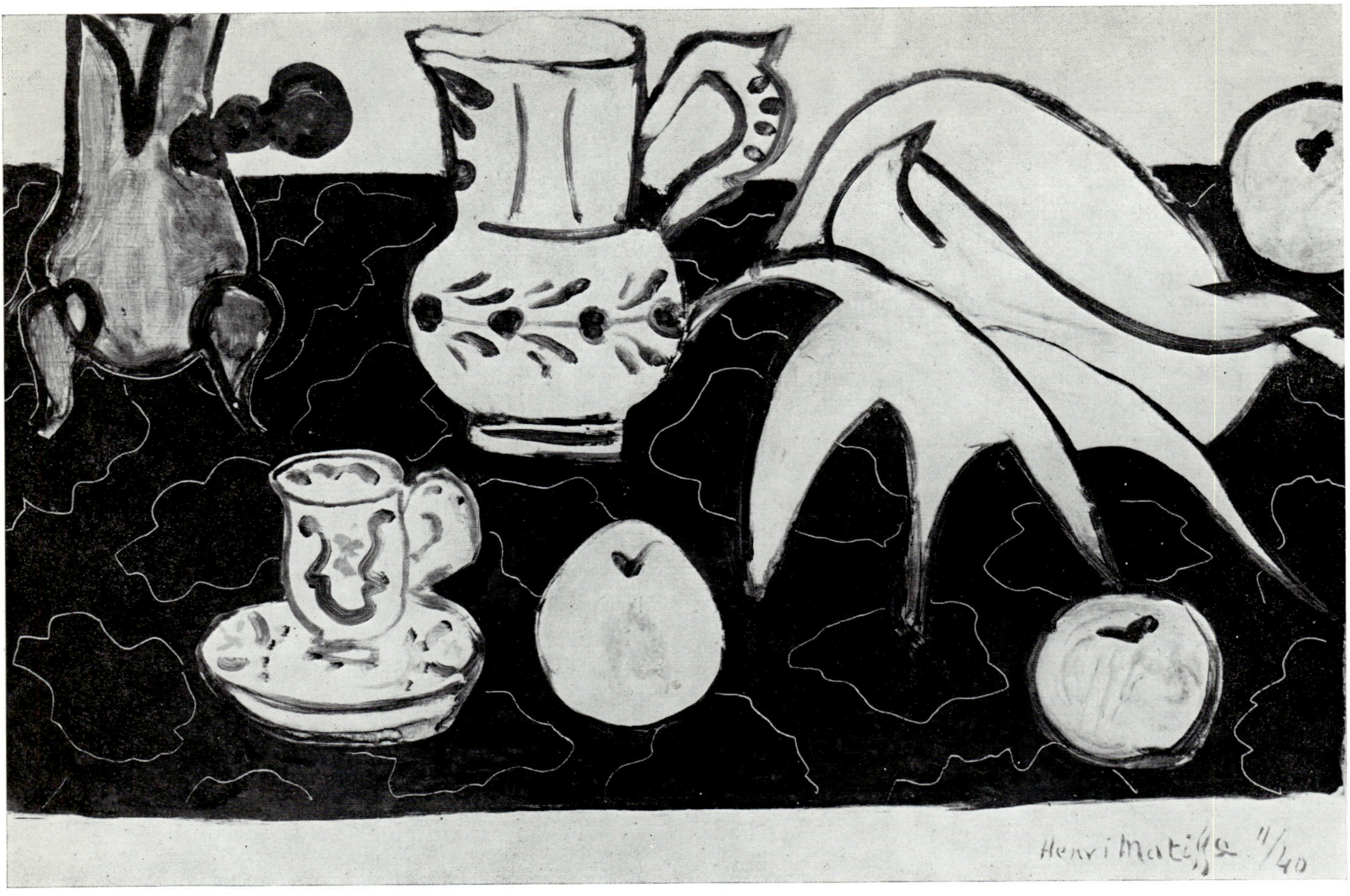

Seashell on Black Marble. 1940
Oil on canvas. $21^1/_4 \times 31^7/_8''$ (54×81 cm)
The Pushkin Museum of Fine Arts, Moscow

least of all *The Dance.* Nevertheless, Matisse — who, above all other painters, strove for joy and clarity — was more drawn to tranquillity and balance in his art. It is therefore quite natural that most of his pictures exude calmness. If they contain any movement, it is most often gentle and charming, as in *Goldfish* (1911, The Pushkin Museum of Fine Arts), a motif that strongly fascinated the artist. In *Goldfish,* the best canvas in an entire series of aquarium still lifes, every artistic device is subordinated to the theme of circular movement.

One could admire the fish swimming in a glass bowl endlessly, but how can they be put into a painting and still keep their charm? First, the red must burn and shine, and in order to achieve this a contrasting supplementary tone or even a combination of tones must be used. The picture has shades of green in it, but nowhere does pure green directly adjoin red, for this clash of color would produce tension and negate the smooth, hypnotic circular movement of the fish. Moreover, black and pink nuances must be added to green for a luxuriant effect. Second, the lines of the picture must be subordinated to a single rhythm and make a pattern in unison with the swimming fish. In this work Matisse persistently repeats ovals and circles at every possible opportunity. He even rejects one of the fundamental principles of Western European painting: the unified viewpoint. He looks at the aquarium from the side and at the table from above; consequently, the basic motif appears in the outline of the tabletop. The pink halo shimmering over the aquarium is a vital effect, for without it the picture would lose its miraculous charm. Another important device is the repetition of the wide circles and ovals in the leaves at the center to form a multitude of minor circles in the area surrounding the fishbowl. Finally all the movement gradually fades away like a distant melody.

When Matisse started to work on a picture he never had any theoretical scheme in mind, but trusted only his instincts. The role of each element in the work was ultimately determined during the process of painting. In *The Artist's Family* (1911, The Hermitage) the composition is again dominated by scarlet, but this color "works" in a completely different way than it does in *Goldfish.* Here it serves to stabilize the entire color scheme, as is dictated by the nature of the scene itself — a peaceful family idyll.

In *The Artist's Family,* Matisse solved the enormously difficult problem of fusing together a variety of different colors and of combining bright unbroken planes with fragmented and extremely diverse oriental patterns. While acknowledging that Persian miniatures had helped him to "go beyond intimate painting," the artist never forgot that in this case he was dealing with a plane of far greater size. During his work on the picture Matisse sent a postcard to Michael Stein, together with a sketch of the composition: "Everything is going well, but since it has not been completed that means nothing; it may not be very logical, but I am not confident of success. This all or nothing is very exhausting." All or nothing — no less — was what Matisse strove for. In depicting his own family — his daughter Marguerite, his sons Jean and Pierre playing draughts, and his wife sewing — Matisse did not actually deal with the conventional devices of a portrait, since his picture was intended to debunk the very idea of a group portrait. (Further, Matisse did not aim at revealing the individual features of his characters, for he was convinced that that could be done more effectively by photography.) With the help of color and its rhythms he produced a work in which an everyday subject was elevated to a solemn, almost hieratic level.

In the composition, oversaturated with color, the checkered pattern of the chessboard (legitimately placed in the center, as if giving the tone to the whole picture) links the oriental carpet, sofa, and the decoration of the walls and fireplace. The main role, however, is assigned to the figures. The most conspicuous spots of color are the boys' shirts and the girl's dress. But striking decorativeness is far from being the only merit of the picture. The sense of festivity permeating *The Artist's Family* reflects the finest and most exalted traits people may have.

One of the most significant examples of twentieth-century portrait painting is *Portrait of the Artist's Wife* (1913, The Hermitage), where, in contrast to *The Artist's Family,* the individuality of Amélie Matisse is brought out more sharply and accurately. Smaller in size and less complicated coloristically, the picture took over a hundred sittings to be completed. Finding in it a charm that he felt was lacking in modern art, Apollinaire called it the masterpiece of the exhibition held in the Salon d'Automne in 1913. Mme Matisse is shown here not as a housewife, as in *The Artist's Family,* but as an elegant Parisian lady. For all the simplicity of its drawing, the details of fashion are rendered very precisely. Perhaps Matisse was even slightly parodying society portraits here; but he could never limit himself to a task of that sort. The woman's face looks like a mask, but what kind of mask? Is it a mask of respectability, or something like one of the African ritual masks that Matisse supposedly had had the chance to see even earlier than Picasso? The woman's sharply delineated features and the strange, enigmatic atmosphere created by the subtle color modulations offset one another. In this picture there is a hint of something phantasmagoric.

The style of the portrait also betrays Matisse's contacts with the Near East, always an important stimulus to his creative work. From his first visit to Biskra in North Africa in 1906, Matisse brought home various works by local craftsmen and eagerly included them in his compositions — such paintings as *Dishes and Fruit on a Red-and-Black Carpet* and *Bouquet,* both in the Hermitage collection. His visits to Tangier in the winters of 1911—12 and 1912—13 marked the beginning of a new stage in his career. The artist later accepted that it was precisely the Moroccan trips that helped him break with Fauvism and discover new links with nature.

In *View from a Window. Tangier* (the left-hand part of the so-called Moroccan triptych, The Pushkin Museum of Fine Arts), all secondary details are omitted, as before, but there are no deliberate deformations to fit the rhythm, as can be seen in *The Red Room* or *Conversation.* A comparison with *Conversation* is quite fitting, since in *View from a Window* Matisse is dealing with a similar theme, except that the human figures have been replaced by two bouquets holding an expressive dialogue, and the landscape has become the focal point. This rapprochement with nature is by no means suggestive of naturalism, for what inspires the artist is the poetic and exalted.

View from a Window. Tangier was painted at the beginning of 1912. Very likely it was in the autumn of the same year, when Matisse was painting *Zorah on the Terrace* and *Entrance to the Casbah* (both in The Pushkin Museum of Fine Arts, and both also for the Moscow collector Morozov, who assembled a collection of Matisses less significant than Shchukin's but nonetheless very valuable), that he decided to unite these three works. It is not quite correct to refer to them as a triptych, because they were not intended to be hung side by side and were not conceived of as an inseparable trio, but rather as a three-part set whose unity is maintained by the variations of a single color. The flowing, subtly modulated blue turns at times into the deep southern sky, shaded trees, or the walls of the houses, and at others into a windowsill or a carpet — each of which then emanates that life-giving blue coolness so much desired in the scorching south. In *Zorah on the Terrace* the light blue is endowed with such power that it even makes the artist omit certain lines that one would think could not be dispensed with at all. Thus, because there is no distinct border between the floor and the walls, the entire scene acquires a semi-fantastic character, as if the woman were floating in some miraculous environment. But what could really have been miraculous about the bare walls of a tiny Moroccan room, or Zorah herself, the "poor maiden of joy" who has been turned into an almost fairy-tale creature by the artist's brush?

In *Arab Coffeehouse* (1913, The Hermitage), one of the most remarkable pictures of the Moroccan cycle, Matisse transforms his concrete, everyday impressions into the highly poetic reality of a painting. Many of the details that passed before the artist's eye are sacrificed to the magical dominance of soft blue. A row of slippers neatly arranged in the lower half of the picture has quite evidently been painted over. We know, too, that when Matisse began the composition it was possible to make out different facial features and that the Moroccans' burnouses were multicolored. Matisse himself said how surprised he was at the ability of the Arabs to contemplate flowers and goldfish for hours on end, and this is what his picture is about. A businessman would either have laughed at or else been exasperated by such a useless waste of time, but for Matisse such a scene conjured up a different, semi-fantastic world, which he approached with deep respect. The Romantic movement had long since become history, but Matisse still retained a romantic attitude toward the East.

The years passed — the First World War, the "mad" twenties, the alarming thirties, then another war unleashed by Germany. Matisse was advised to flee overseas, but he refused to leave France. The Nazi invasion caught him in Paris and only with difficulty did he reach Nice two months later.

In Nice, which he had long made his chief residence, Matisse started to paint the still life *Seashell on Black Marble* (1940, The Pushkin Museum of Fine Arts). After at least thirty sessions of intense work the seventy-year-old master completed the canvas to his full satisfaction. The jug, coffeepot, and fruit are the beautiful, familiar items he had already painted hundreds of times before. Only the seashell is new. But wasn't this the reason why the picture was painted? The huge seashell is at once dead and somehow strangely alive. There is something threatening in its brilliant pink surface and spurs, which contrast sharply with the black marble. Although the various items here are assembled without any thematic sense (why should the shell be placed next to the apples and the jug?), they are all beautifully etched against the black marble. The artist seeks a number of plastic analogies, comparing the patterns on the marble and on the cup, the leg of the coffeepot, and the spurs of the seashell.

The year 1940 was drawing to an end and France was entering a period of long hardships and trials as Matisse was painting *Seashell on Black Marble.* Should he have begun a tragic picture at this time? He had never painted such things. His talent was of a completely different nature: his art had always served not as a mirror for, but as a counterweight to, misfortune. *Seashell* both resembles and differs from his previous still lifes. Though permeated with a sense of alarm, it still shines with the unfading golden light of hope and expresses the artist's admiration for the beauty of the surrounding world and for everything that has been created by other artists and folk craftsmen. There is nothing allegorical in the painting. As always, Matisse painted from nature; for him the meaning of art was a direct contact with objects. But his art is not enclosed, it is always addressed to life and to people. That is why this set of heterogeneous objects conveys a breath of life that flows beyond the walls of the artist's studio and strikes a response in his soul. The objects also embody beauty and joie de vivre, the antithesis of chaos.

Matisse had another thirteen years to live, and during this time he was to turn to easel painting less and less often. He was to discover new spheres of endeavor for himself — from gouache cutouts to the creation of the Chapelle du Rosaire for the Dominican nuns in Vence, with its unique murals, stained-glass panels, and other decorations. New themes and images appeared in his art, but its essence — deeply human and spiritually clear — remained unchanged.

Albert Kostenevich

BIOGRAPHICAL OUTLINE

1869 Born on December 31 in Le Cateau-Cambrésis (Nord)

1890 Begins painting

1891 Enters the Académie Julian in Paris

1892 Enrolled in the studio of Gustave Moreau at the Ecole des Beaux-Arts

1893—94 Paints copies in The Louvre

1896 Exhibited at the Salon de la Société Nationale des Beaux-Arts. Elected an Associate Member of the Salon

1897 Meets Camille Pissarro. *La Desserte* exhibited at the Salon

1898 Marries Amélie Parayre. Travels to London, Corsica, and Toulouse

1899 Leaves the Ecole des Beaux-Arts and attends the Académie Carriere

1903 Exhibited at Berthe Weil's, the Salon des Indépendants, and the Salon d'Automne

1904 First one-man exhibition at Ambroise Vollard's. Spends the summer in Saint-Tropez with Paul Signac and Henri-Edmond Cross

1905 Spends the summer in Collioure with André Derain. Exhibited at the Salon d'Automne with Derain, Maurice de Vlaminck, Albert Marquet, and others

1906 *The Joy of Living* exhibited at the Salon des Indépendants

1908 "Notes of a Painter" published in *La Grande Revue*

1910 *The Dance* and *Music* exhibited at the Salon d'Automne. Travels to Spain

1911 Trip to Russia

1912—13 Stay in Morocco

1916 Journey to Nice

1925 Trip to Italy

1927 Receives the Carnegie Prize

1932 Finishes *The Dance* for the Barnes Foundation in Merion, Pennsylvania. Completes a series of etchings for *Poésies* by Stéphane Mallarmé

1942 A series of drawings, *Themes and Variations*

1947 Gouache collages for the album *Jazz*

1951 Inauguration of the Chapelle du Rosaire in Vence, designed and painted by Matisse

1954 Dies on November 3 in Nice

VIEW OF COLLIOURE. 1905

Oil on canvas. $23^3/_8 \times 28^3/_4$" (59.5 × 73 cm)

The Hermitage, Leningrad

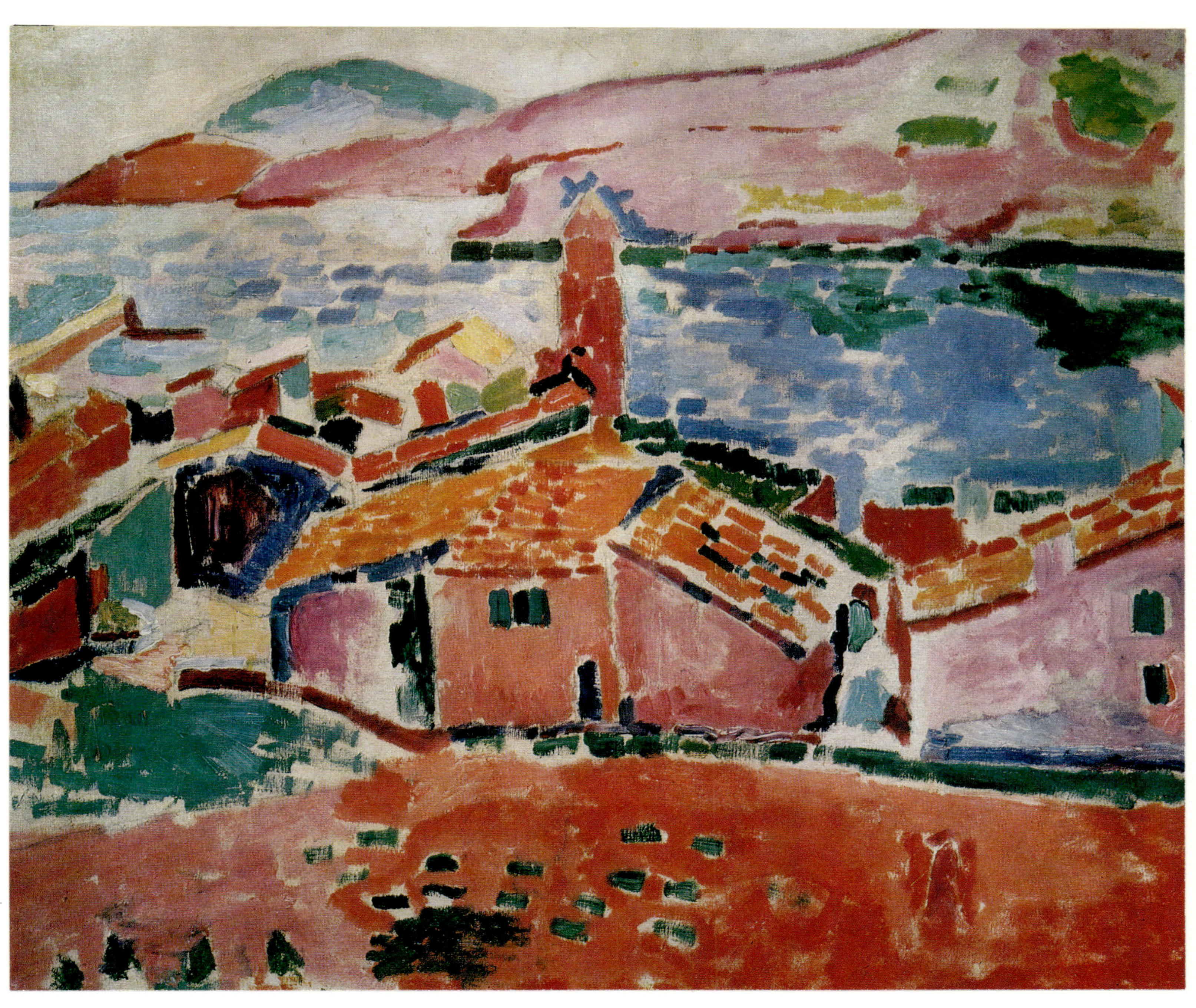

DISHES AND FRUIT ON A RED-AND-BLACK CARPET. 1906

Oil on canvas. 24 × 29 1/2" (61 × 75 cm)
The Hermitage, Leningrad

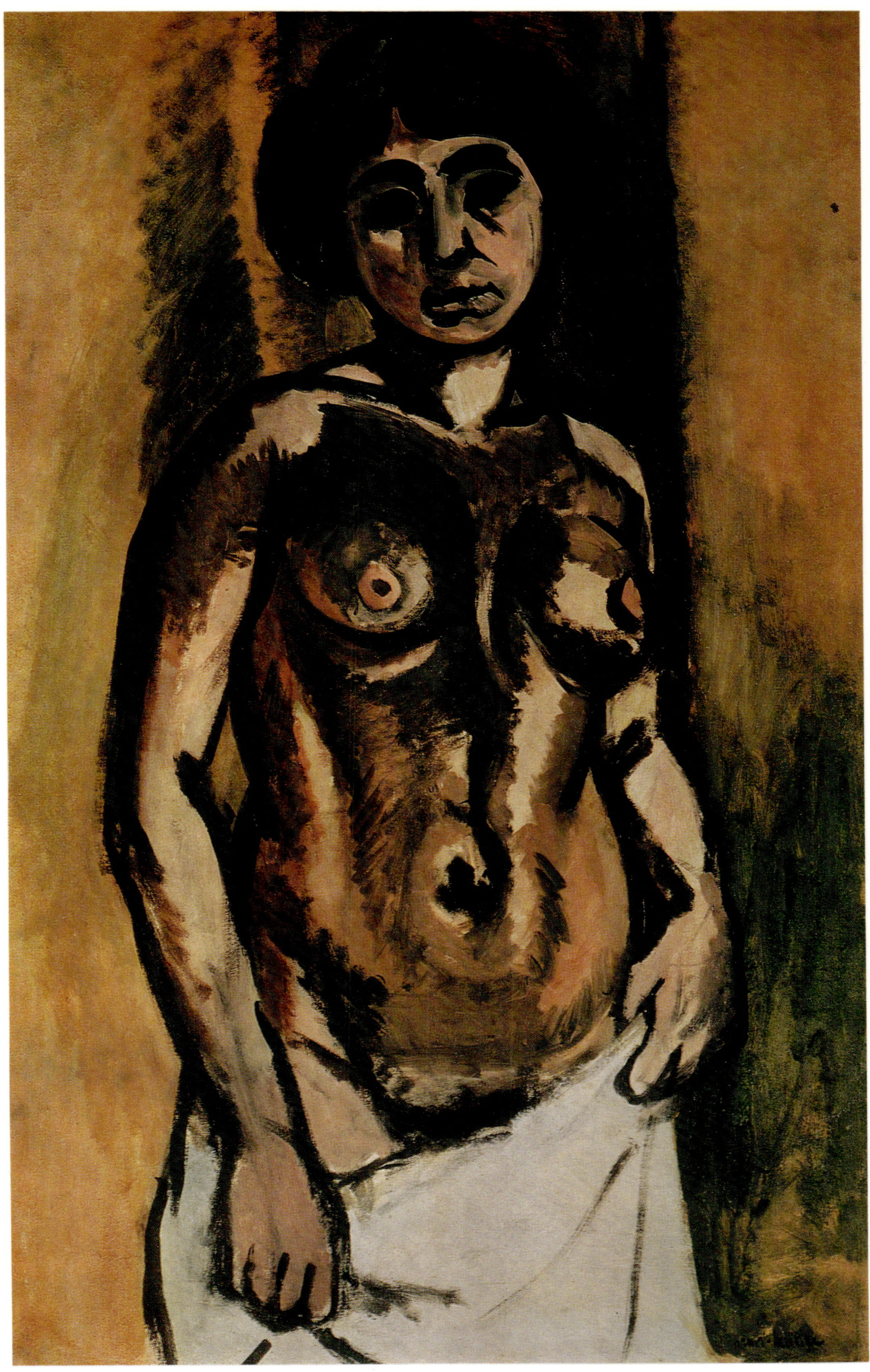

THE RED ROOM
(*LA DESSERTE*. HARMONY IN RED). 1908–1909
Oil on canvas. $70^7/_8 \times 86^5/_8$″ (180 × 220 cm)
The Hermitage, Leningrad

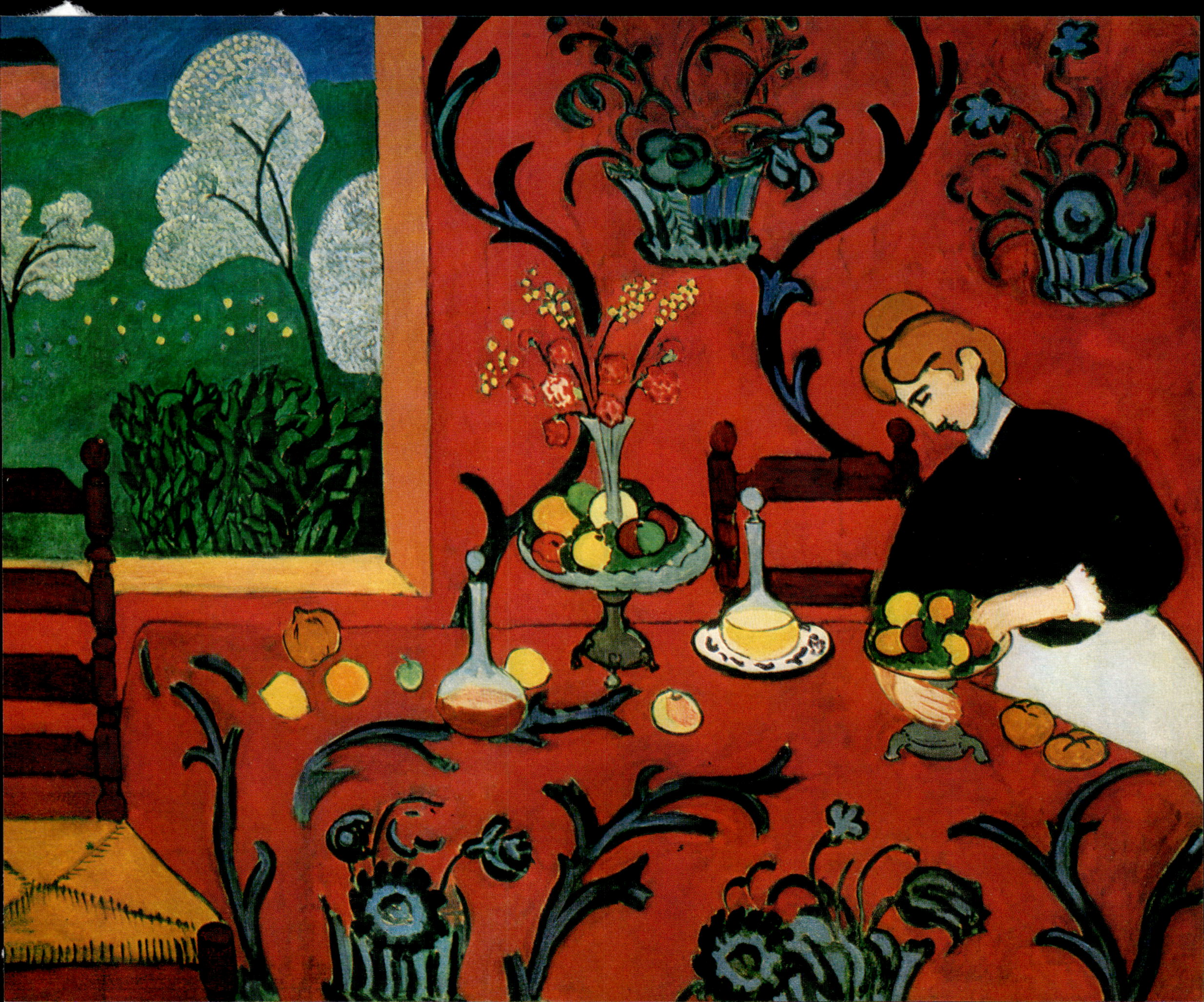

Англ. яз.

BLUE TABLECLOTH. 1909

Oil on canvas. $34^5/_8 \times 46^1/_4''$ (88 × 118 cm)
The Hermitage, Leningrad

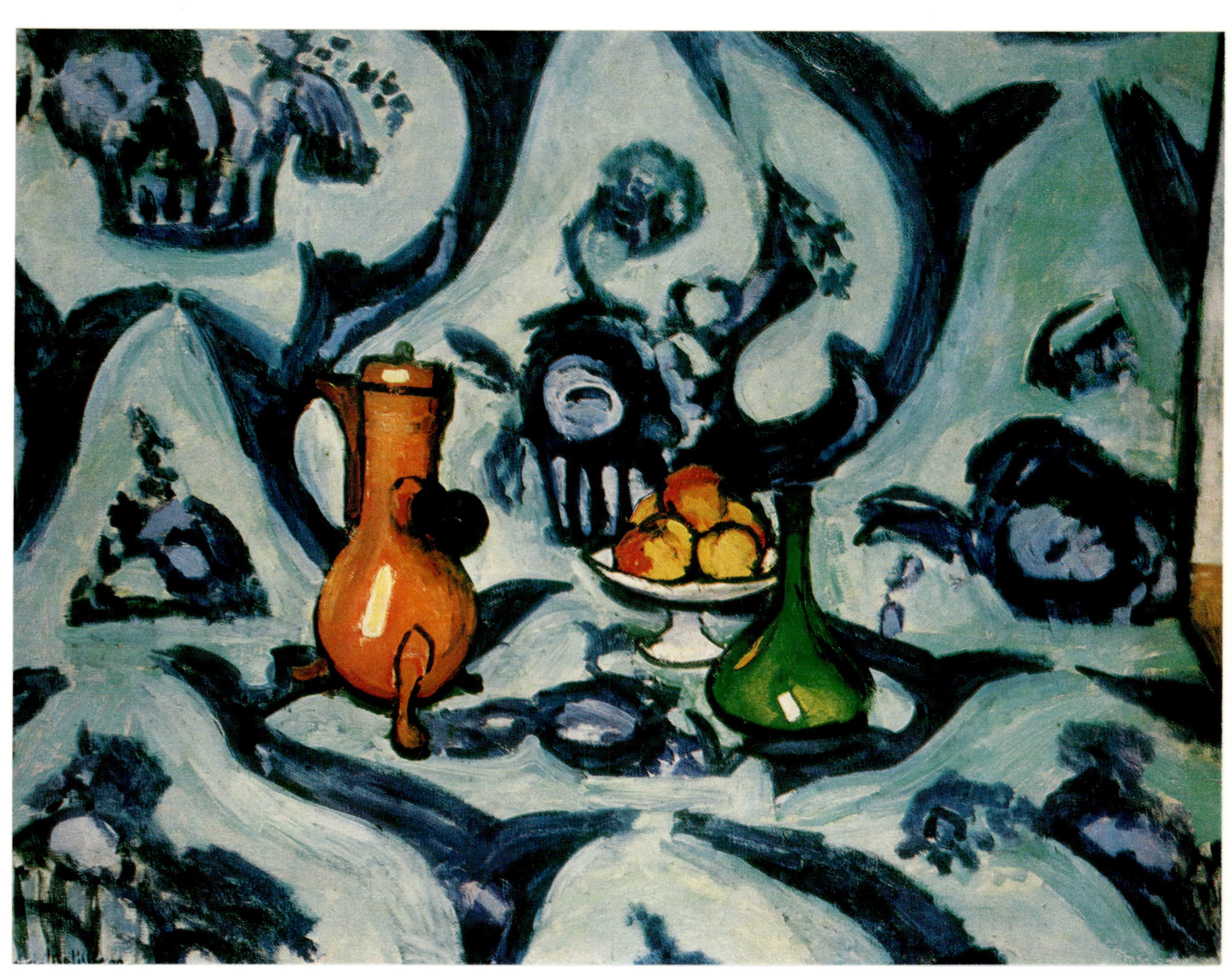

SPANISH WOMAN WITH TAMBOURINE. 1909

Oil on canvas. $36^1/_4 \times 28^3/_4''$ (92 × 73 cm)

The Pushkin Museum of Fine Arts, Moscow

Англ. яз.

CONVERSATION. 1909

Oil on canvas. $69^5/_8 \times 85^1/_2$″ (177×217 cm)
The Hermitage, Leningrad

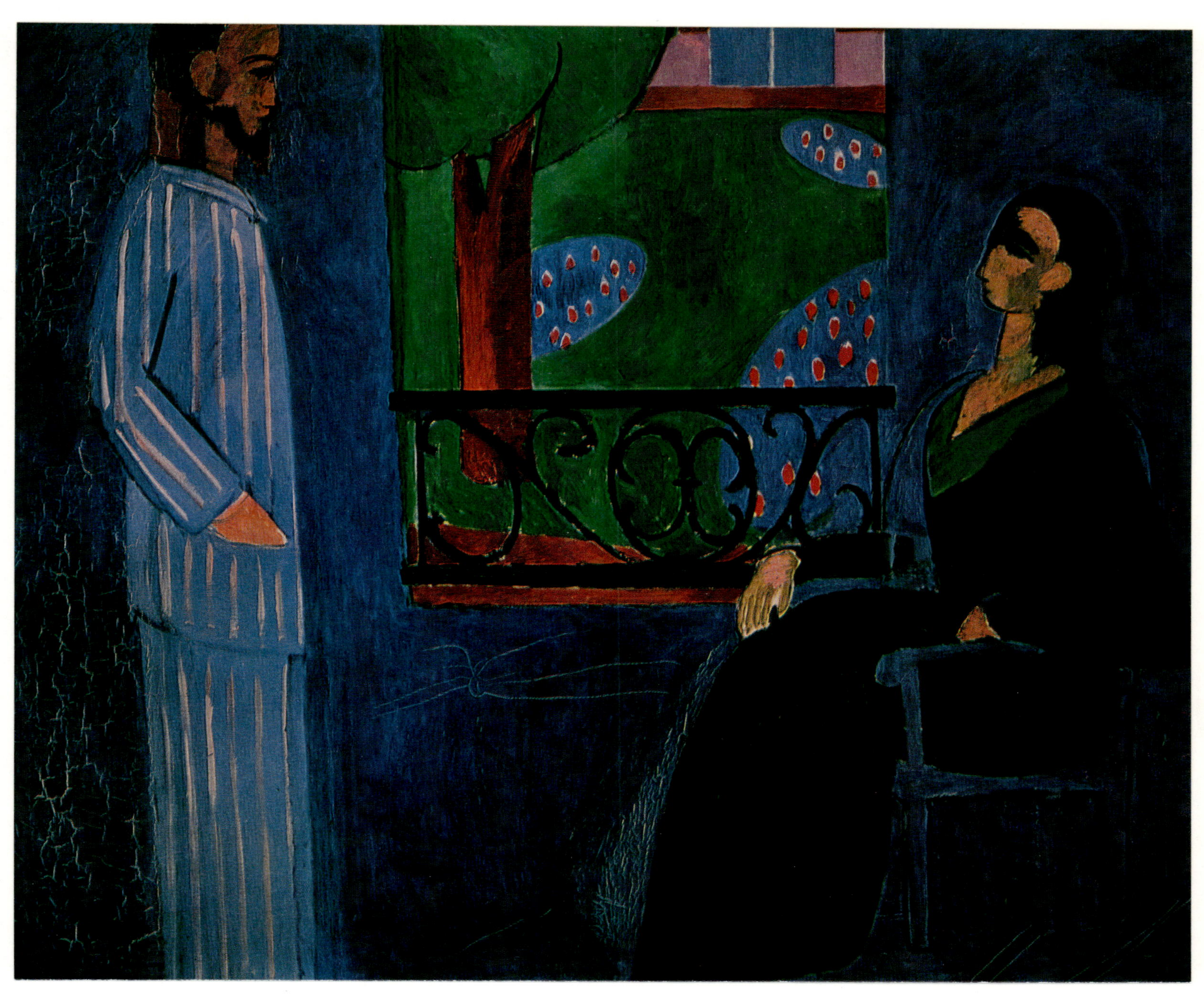

THE DANCE. 1910
Oil on canvas. $102^{3}/_{8} \times 154''$ (260×391 cm)
The Hermitage, Leningrad

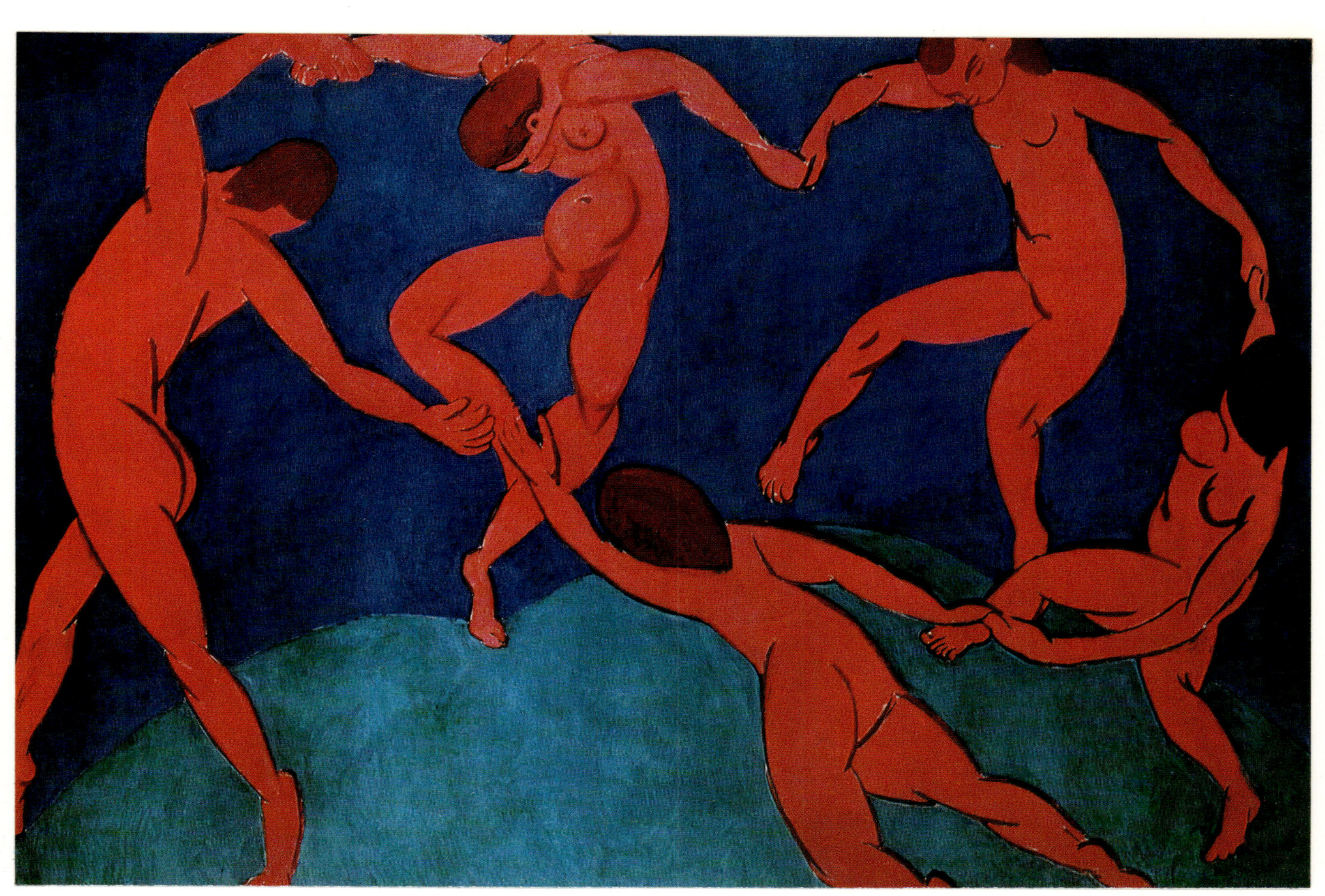

MUSIC. 1910

Oil on canvas. $102^3/_8 \times 153^1/_8''$ (260 × 389 cm)

The Hermitage, Leningrad

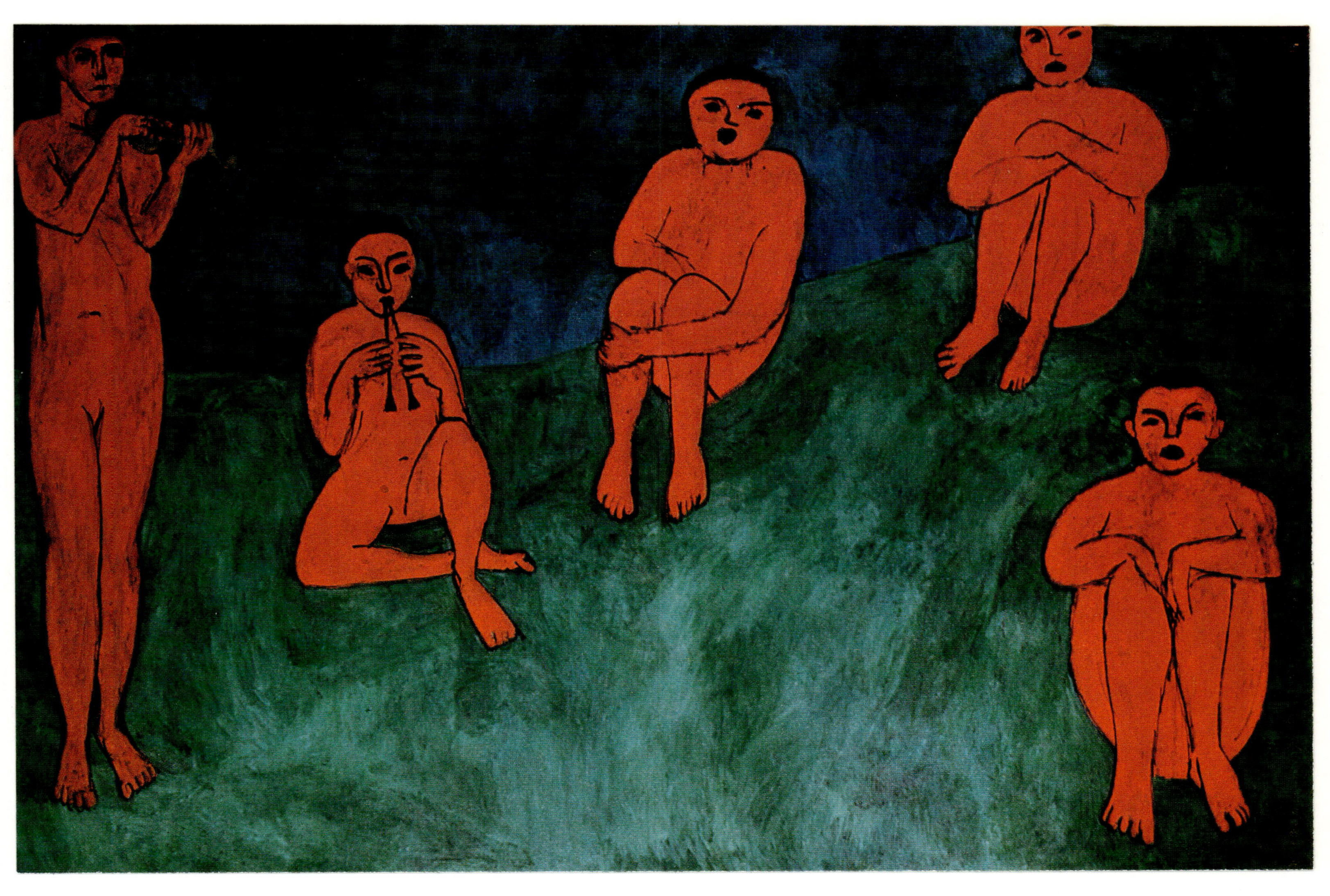

GOLDFISH. 1911

Oil on canvas. $57^7/_8 \times 38^5/_8''$ (147 × 98 cm)
The Pushkin Museum of Fine Arts, Moscow

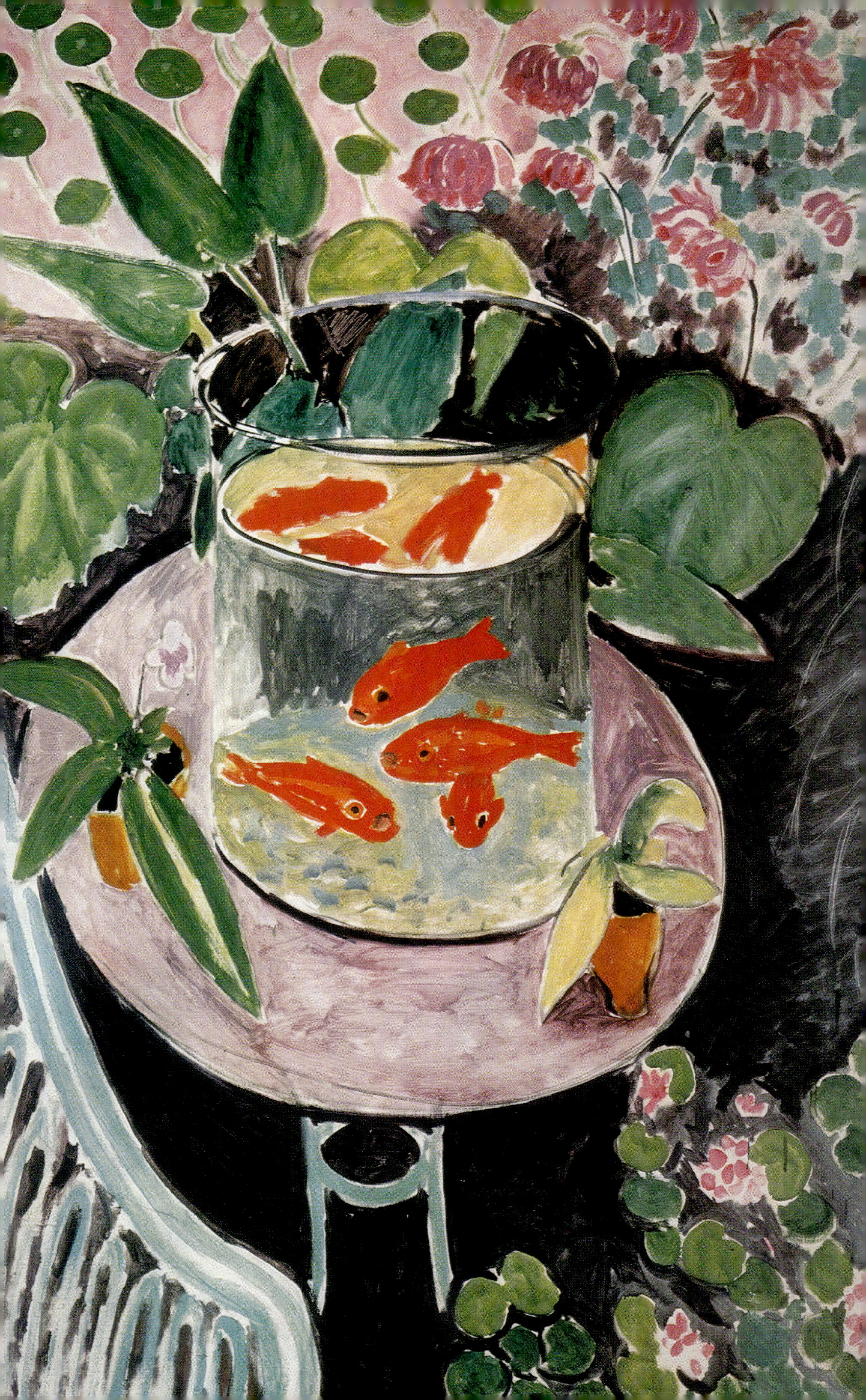

Англ.іяъ.

THE ARTIST'S FAMILY. 1911

Oil on canvas. $56^3/_8 \times 76^3/_8$" (143 × 194 cm)

The Hermitage, Leningrad

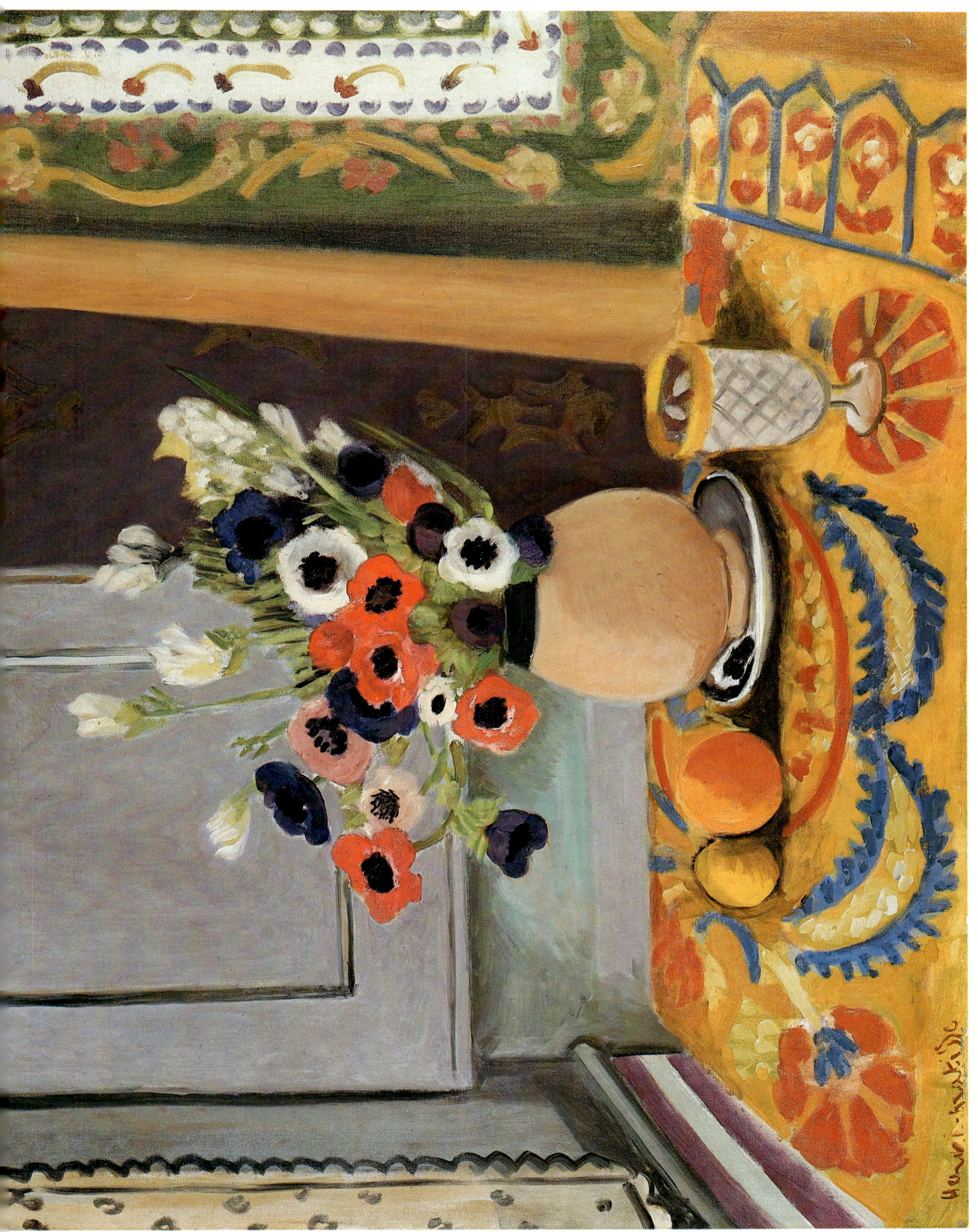

AUGUST 1987

SUNDAY	MONDAY	TUESDAY	WEDNESDAY	THURSDAY	FRIDAY	SATURDAY
						1
2	3	4	5	6	7	8
9	10	11	12	13	14	15
16	17	18	19	20	21	22
23	24	25	26	27	28	29

S	M	T	W	T	F	S
			1	2	3	4
5	6	7	8	9	10	11
12	13	14	15	16	17	18
19	20	21	22	23	24	25
26	27	28	29	30	31	

S	M	T	W	T	F	S
		1	2	3	4	5
6	7	8	9	10	11	12
13	14	15	16	17	18	19
20	21	22	23	24	25	26
27	28	29	30			

Англ. яз.

THE ARTIST'S STUDIO. 1911

Oil on canvas. $71^1/_4 \times 87''$ (181×221 cm)
The Pushkin Museum of Fine Arts, Moscow

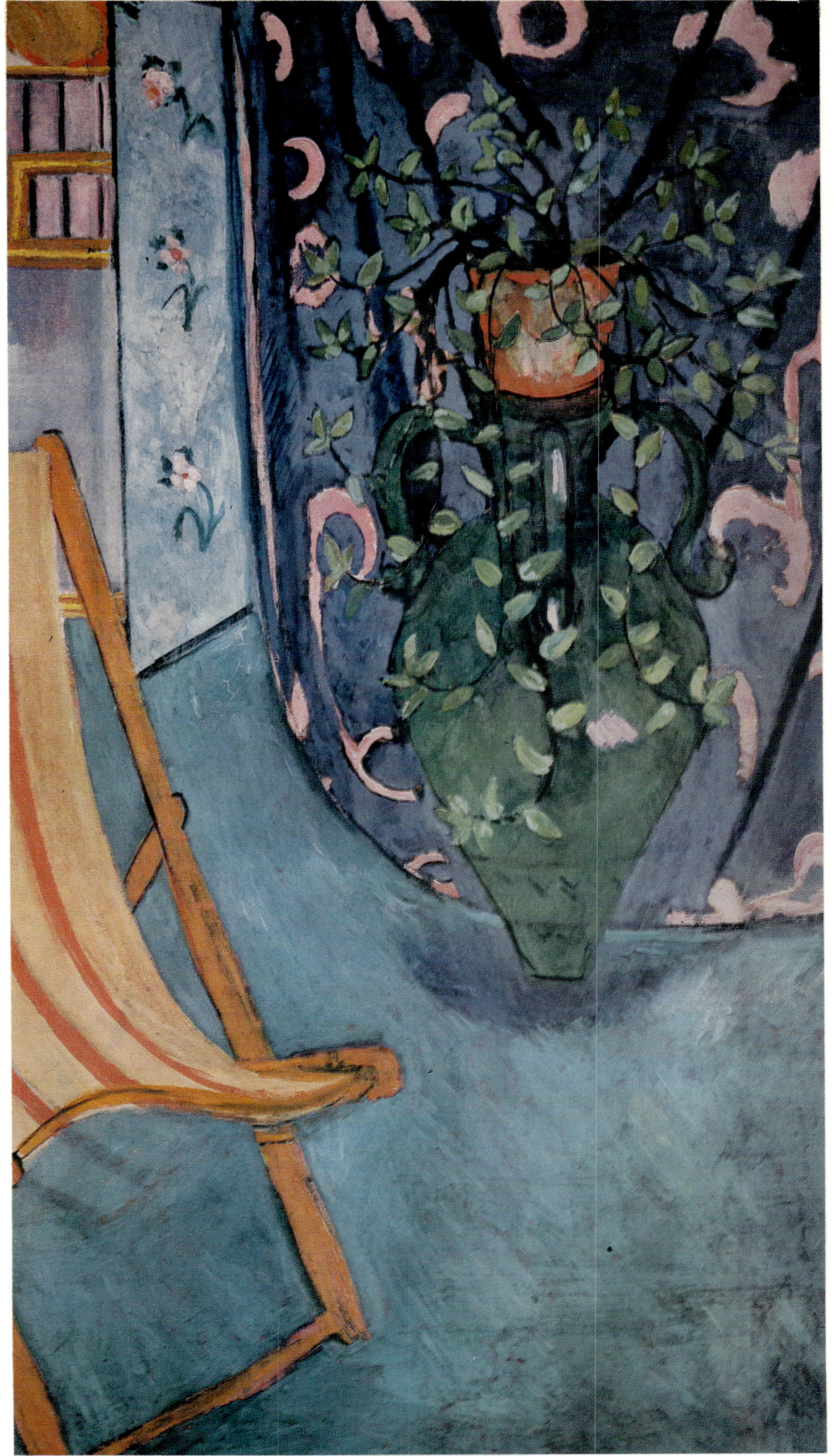

PORTRAIT OF THE ARTIST'S WIFE. 1913
Oil on canvas. $57^7/_8 \times 38^1/_4$" (145 × 97 cm)
The Hermitage, Leningrad

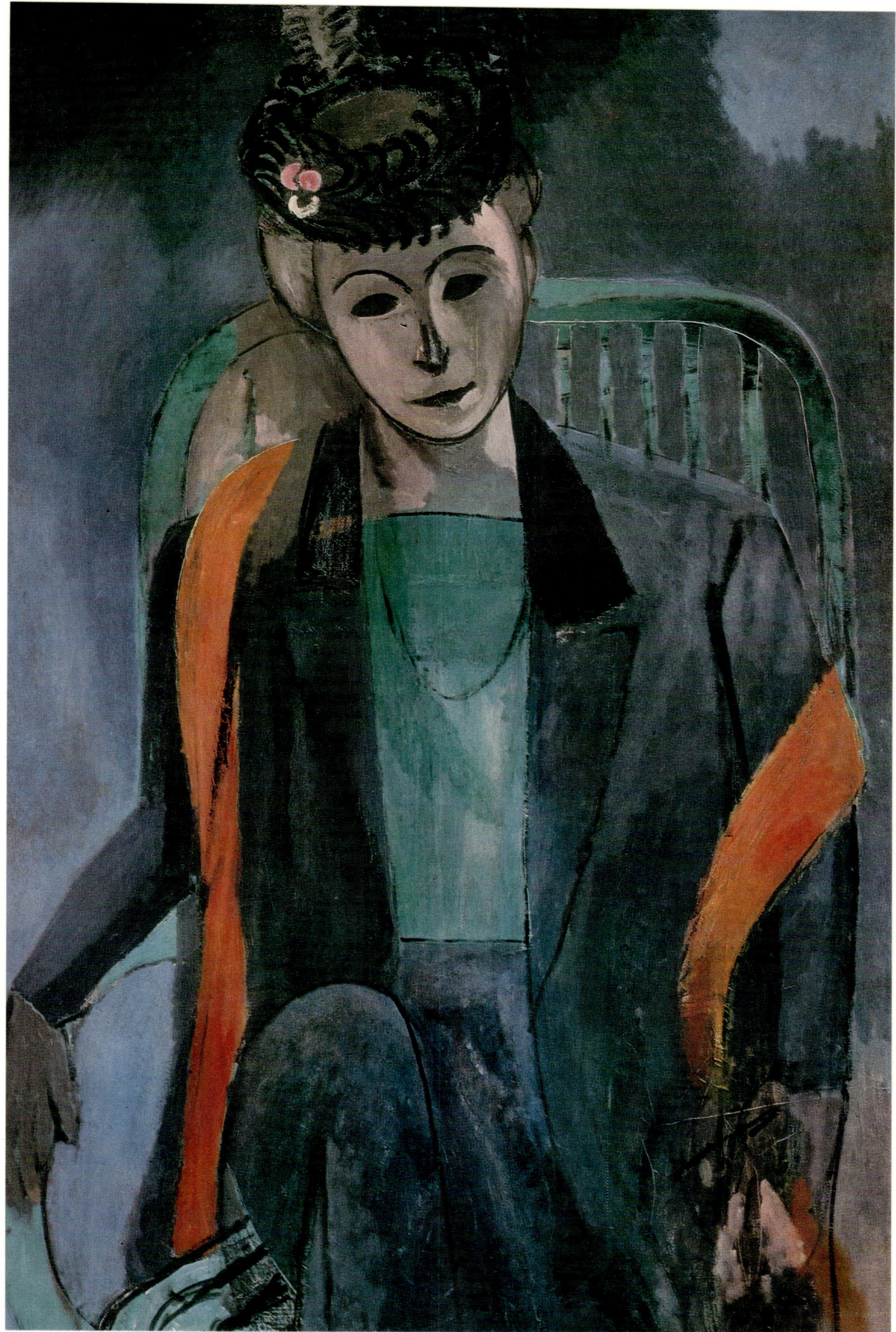

ARAB COFFEEHOUSE. 1913

Size colors on canvas. $69^3/_8 \times 82^5/_8''$ (176×210 cm)

The Hermitage, Leningrad

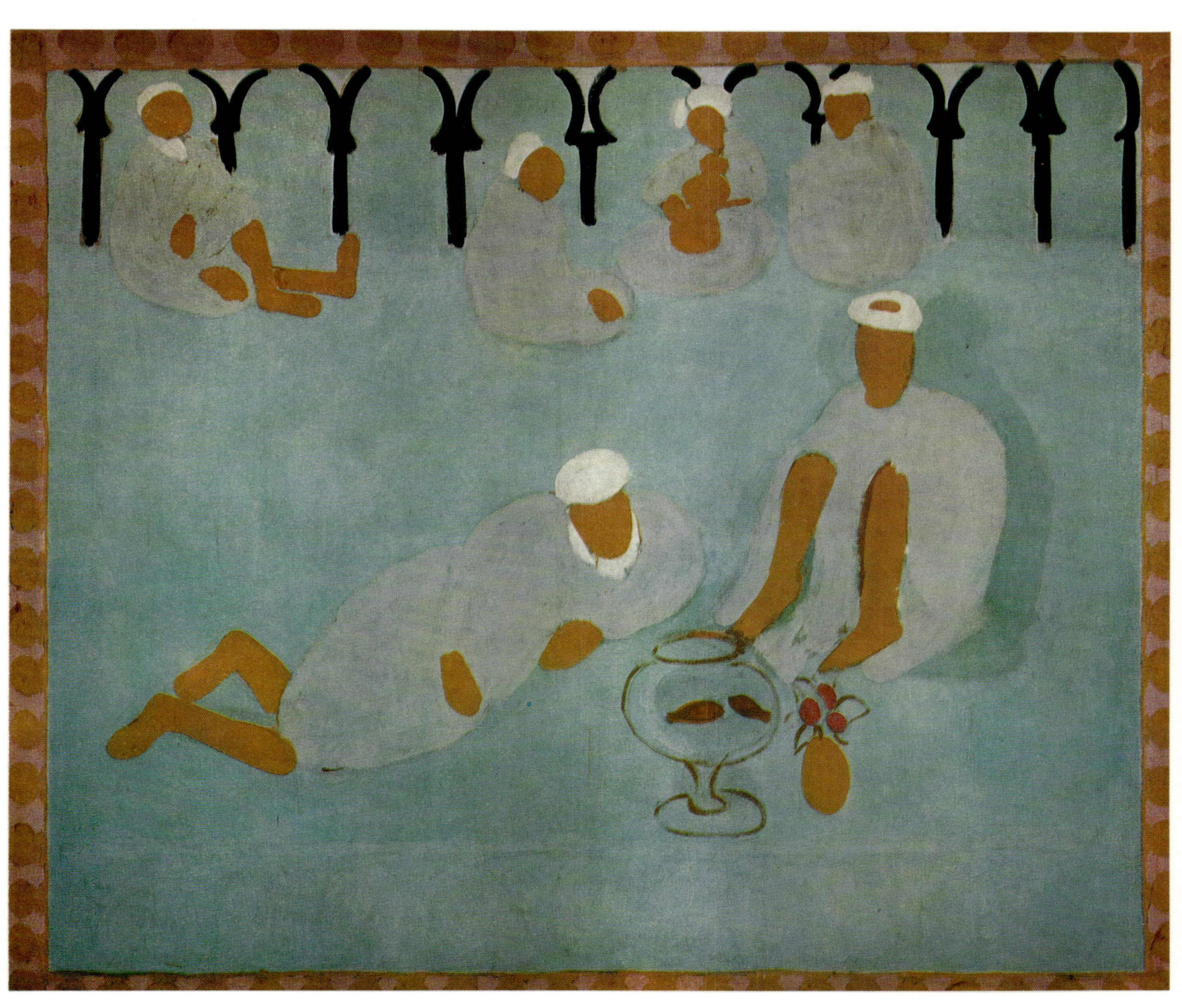

PORTRAIT OF LYDIA DELECTORSKAYA. 1947

Oil on canvas. $25^3/_8 \times 19^1/_4$″ (64.3×49.7 cm)

The Hermitage, Leningrad

On the jacket:
Bouquet (Vase with Two Handles). 1907
Oil on canvas. $29^{1}/_{4} \times 24''$ (74×61 cm)
The Hermitage, Leningrad

АНРИ МАТИСС
Альбом (на английском языке)
ИЗДАТЕЛЬСТВО „АВРОРА". ЛЕНИНГРАД. 1981
Изд. № 2636. Printed and bound in the USSR